WILL YOU NOT REVIVE US AGAIN?

Psalms 83-85

and the urgent call to seek God in a church facing judgment

LEE GATISS

Will you not revive us again? Psalms 83–85 and the urgent call to seek God in a church facing judgment

by Lee Gatiss

© Church Society 2025
Church Society
Ground Floor, Centre Block
Hille Business Estate,
132 St Albans Road
Watford WD24 4AE, UK

Tel +44 (0)1923 255410
www.churchsociety.org
admin@churchsociety.org

Unless otherwise stated, all Scripture quotations are taken from The Holy Bible, New International Version. Copyright © 1973, 1978, 1984, 2011 by Biblica, Inc. Used by permission. All rights reserved.

All rights reserved. Except as may be permitted by the Copyright Act, no part of this publication may be reproduced in any form or by any means without prior permission from the publisher.

Readers are reminded that the views expressed by the author of the book do not necessarily represent those of Church Society.

Printed in the UK
ISBN: 978-1-0685705-6-8

Church Society

EQUIPPING GOD'S
PEOPLE TO LIVE
GOD'S WORD

Contents

Introduction 5

Facing the Enemies: Psalm 83 9

Longing for God: Psalm 84 30

Praying for Glory: Psalm 85 49

Introduction

Back in 2022, as I was editing Tim Chester's excellent new commentary on Psalms for the Hodder Bible Commentary, I was particularly struck by Psalms 83, 84, and 85. They gripped me, jumping off the page at me to assert their relevance for the church in England right now. I found it fascinating to see how they might relate and hang together as a group, and have become convinced that they proclaim a vital message for us as Christians today.

I have been pondering them since then, on retreat, in staff meetings and prayer meetings, for articles in Crossway magazine, in talks at the Bishop of Ebbsfleet's regional conferences, and for the Bible by the Beach convention in Eastbourne. I thought now might be a good time to commit my reflections to paper, especially as there is a growing interest in the subject of revival across the UK.

These three psalms come from a time when God's people were under threat—politically, spiritually, and morally. They are raw, honest, and deeply relevant for any generation feeling the ache of decline and the longing for God to act. I think now is such a time.

I hope you will enjoy reflecting on these psalms with me in this booklet, even if you don't entirely share my understanding of the times we live in or what I think God is doing right now. Only God's word is unerring and infallible so I make no claim to that sort of inspiration for my own thoughts that have been prayerfully provoked by it. Though I hope that you will join me in praying for God to reform and renew us, using the words of these astonishing psalms.

In the Anglican Book of Common Prayer, one prays through the whole book of

Psalms every month. Psalms 83-85 appear in the reading cycle on Day 16. So whether you follow that lectionary yourself or not, why not make a note in your diary to pray every 16th day of the month, for God to revive us again? Who knows what he might do in response to our urgent and heartfelt prayers?

LEE GATISS

Cambridge

16th June 2025

Facing the Enemies

Psalm 83

We have to be realistic about the trememdous hostility of the world towards God, and his church today.

It's hard not to be sombre about the state of the Church of England at the moment, and the state of the Church in England. At a national level, in the established church, there has been a massive failure of due process and good leadership, and there is a gigantic deficit of good theology, healthy church discipline, and acceptable safeguarding practice.

Instead of "Repent and believe the good

news!" as Jesus preached (Mark 1:15), the corporate messaging nowadays seems to be that one can believe in anything and need repent of nothing – all with God's blessing.

About 10% of General Synod are members of Church Society, but we are not represented at the senior levels of the church in anything like a proportional way. We have one bishop reflective of our classic Anglican theology, out of about 120. Meanwhile, there are renewed attempts to force us out again, by those who hate our teaching and our love for God's word.

This would of course also fatally weaken the coalition against the current revisionist campaigns, and see the ever-onward march of heresy empty our churches even more. This would be cheered on by various groups in our culture and society who would like nothing more than to see us and our gospel consigned to the dustbin of history.

Common sense seems rare in the public square, and the Christian faith which built our civilisation over two millennia is often patronised, treated condescendingly, and pilloried by those with little understanding of it. People would rather stay at home and watch TV or play sports on a Sunday, instead of joining us to worship and adore Jesus, the saviour of the world.

Doomed, defeated, and depressed?

All this puts me in mind of Psalm 83, written when it seemed that God's people were doomed, defeated, and depressed. Look at how Asaph the psalmist prayed to God in his situation:

Psalm 83

A song. A psalm of Asaph.

> O God, do not remain silent;
> > do not turn a deaf ear,
> > do not stand aloof, O God.
> See how your enemies growl,
> > how your foes rear their heads.
> With cunning they conspire against your people;
> > they plot against those you cherish.
> "Come," they say, "let us destroy them as a nation,
> > so that Israel's name is remembered no more."
>
> With one mind they plot together;
> > they form an alliance against you—
> the tents of Edom and the Ishmaelites,
> > of Moab and the Hagrites,
> Byblos, Ammon and Amalek,
> Philistia, with the people of Tyre.
> Even Assyria has joined them
> > to reinforce Lot's descendants.
> Do to them as you did to Midian,

>   as you did to Sisera and Jabin at the river Kishon,
> who perished at Endor
>   and became like dung on the ground.
> Make their nobles like Oreb and Zeeb,
>   all their princes like Zebah and Zalmunna,
> who said, "Let us take possession
>   of the pasturelands of God."
>
> Make them like tumbleweed, my God,
>   like chaff before the wind.
> As fire consumes the forest
>   or a flame sets the mountains ablaze,
> so pursue them with your tempest
>   and terrify them with your storm.
> Cover their faces with shame, LORD,
>   so that they will seek your name.
> May they ever be ashamed and dismayed;
>   may they perish in disgrace.
> Let them know that you, whose name is the LORD—
>   that you alone are the Most High over all the earth.

An alliance of enemies from all around had conspired with cunning to plot against the nation. Verses 5-8 describe their conspiracy: "With one mind they plot together" it says, listing the many enemies all around who were assaulting God's covenant people at the time.

They growl, menacingly. They put aside all their differences, like Pontius Pilate and King Herod, to bring down God and his people (see Luke 23:12).

Early church fathers such as Jerome (342-420) saw these crafty adversaries of God's people as a prophetic picture of false teachers abusing the church. The medieval commentator Thomas Aquinas (1225-1274) saw them as insolent external foes such as persecution and unbelief, attacking the church.[1]

The Reformer, John Calvin (1509-1564) commented on this psalm: "But it is, as it

---

1 See Tim Chester, *Psalms 42-89* (The Hodder Bible Commentary; London: Hodder & Stoughton, 2024), 357.

*At the present day,
none are more furiously
mad against us than
counterfeit Christians*

were, the destiny of the Church, not only to be assailed by external enemies, but to suffer far greater trouble at the hands of false brethren. At the present day, none are more furiously mad against us than counterfeit Christians."[2]

And the psalmist cries out in the midst of this bombardment:

> O God, do not remain silent;
> do not turn a deaf ear,
> do not stand aloft, O God…

Why are you so quiet, God? We know that one day Jesus will return and appear in the glory of his Father, and sit on the throne of judgment. He will come again to judge the living and the dead, as the Creed says. But right now, he often seems to be silent, while we are all led like lambs to the slaughter.

What strange providence is this? Where is God in it all? When will his silence and our

---

2 John Calvin, *Commentary on the Book of Psalms* (trans. James Anderson; Bellingham, WA: Logos Bible Software, 2010), 344–345.

suffering come to an end? Do not stand aloft, O God!

I often find myself praying along just such lines at this time. I want the Church of England nationally to know that God is God, and to honour his word, when it seems that it has been sidelined and ignored and attacked. And when church attendances have quite understandably plummeted across the country over the last few decades.

When I first got ordained, 72% of people described themselves as Christian in the national census. Now it's well under half. And we have stagnation and decline, confusion and division, in our land, as a result of all this "freedom" from Christian influence. Other more malign and secular influences have not made us a happier nation, as we've moved away from God.

"Come on, God – please *do* something about it!" It is disheartening and exhausting to be constantly on the defensive against

... we have stagnation and decline, confusion and division, in our land, as a result of all this "freedom" from Christian influence.

all kinds of pressures, and it is natural for a Christian heart to turn to God, and ask for divine relief.

Who are these enemies in Psalm 83:5-8?

> With one mind they plot together;
> > they form an alliance against you–
> the tents of Edom and the Ishmaelites,
> > of Moab and the Hagrites,
> Byblos, Ammon and Amalek,
> > Philistia, with the people of Tyre.
> Even Assyria has joined them
> > to reinforce Lot's descendants.

They are idolatrous cults and sects, and historic tribal enemies of Israel. They are evil empires like Ammon and Amalek who plot its destruction. They are centres of commerce and trade like Tyre, which want wealth and power and influence. They are great powers like Assyria who want to dominate the world and bring everyone under its sway.

These worldly powers will forever be opposed to God and his people. Or as Psalm 2 said, they gather together against the Lord, and his Messiah (Psalm 2:2).

The Psalmist prays they would all be defeated, just as God defeated his enemies in the books of Joshua and Judges. The names may not be familiar to you. They are long-defeated opponents of God: Sisera and Jabin, Oreb and Zeeb, Zebah and Zalmunna.

These people said, verse 12, "Let us take possession of the pasturelands of God." They saw something of God's and they wanted it. They moved against it. But ultimately they failed. And that's maybe why their names are not so familiar. Their names have perished – who has ever heard of them?! – but God's name has not, and his covenant people continue to flourish around the world.

Let them know your name

Do to our current opponents what you did to those guys — that's what the Psalmist is saying to God in the midst of all these assaults. God, you totally trampled over your enemies in the past, so you could do so again with our enemies today. "Make them like tumbleweed, my God, like chaff before the wind." You can do it. Go on!

I'm sure they were all very scary and impressive names in their day. People were frightened of Edom, and intimidated by Sisera. Amalek struck fear in their hearts, and Tyre filled them with awe. Like the names Putin and Trump and Xi or Ayotollah Khamenei, or Musk and Bezos and Zuckerberg.

But to God, these names are nothing, whatever they may try against him, whatever conspiracies they might be backing. The memory of them will fade.

Look at them all, Lord. Those oppressive regimes that persecute your people and censor the gospel.

Look at them, Lord. The money men and money women, who don't care about truth and justice, but only want to suck us dry for profit or pursue their own vanities.

Look at them, Lord. Pushing their ideologies, dominating the discussion, pushing the word of truth aside as if it was a bronze age relic so easily ignored. Look at the proud, scoffing, cultural superiority of those who want to drag the church away from Christ and devotion to his word. The pressure they exert on your precious people to turn away from your voice.

God, who has so often put his enemies to flight and rescued his poor trembling sheep out of the jaws of wolves, is not without the power to do the same again.

It can sound a bit militaristic or violent, some of this. But of course, it isn't calling for a vengeful and violent insurrection of Christians to overthrow these dominating

God, who has so often put his enemies to flight and rescued his poor trembling sheep out of the jaws of wolves, is not without the power to do the same again.

powers. There is no support here for a crusade, for us to take up arms against those who hate Christ and the gospel, and bring them to heel. That is not our way.[3]

It's a call for God to act, a yearning for him to be honoured. He could blow these people out like a tiny candle, in a puff of smoke. If he wanted to.

But note what the Psalmist wants above all. From verse 16…

> Cover their faces with shame, LORD,
> so that they will seek your name.
> May they ever be ashamed and dismayed;
> may they perish in disgrace.
> Let them know that you, whose name is the LORD–
> that you alone are the Most High over all the earth.

The big thing? He wants everyone to know God, to seek him, and to glorify him. Cov-

---

3 See Lee Gatiss, *Fight Valiantly: Contending for the Faith against False Teaching in the Church* (London: Church Society, 2022), 133-135 on how most Christians have historically opposed the use of force in religious matters.

er their faces with shame *so that* they will seek your name. Let them know that *you*, whose *name* is the LORD, that you alone are the Most High over all the earth.

What the Psalmist most wants is for these enemies to know God. To seek his name. That means they must be shamed, for their opposition to him. But dismay that leads to repentance and a knowledge of the truth is good dismay. As Charles Spurgeon said, "shame has often weaned men from their idols, and set them upon seeking the Lord."[4] Bring them to nothing Lord, so they may be brought to you.

Why not do it now, Lord? Why in your providence do you wait?

We have to be realistic about the tremendous hostility of the world towards God, and his church today. But that hostile mob is bound to fail dismally, because Christ – the name above all names – will be victo-

---

4 Charles H. Spurgeon, *The Treasury of David* (3 vols.; Peabody: Hendrickson, 1990), 2:422.

rious.

Blow them away like chaff in the wind, or convert them to true faith, Lord!

We know that one day, at the *name* of Jesus, every knee will bow (Philippians 2:10). Until that day, we know already that "all authority in heaven and earth" has been given to Jesus. So our role in the overthrow of these powers ranged against him, is to baptise people in the *name* of the Father, the Son, and the Holy Spirit, teaching them to obey all that he has commanded (Matthew 28:18-20).

That's how it starts.

I often want to pray like the psalmist: "Lord, remember England! Remember the Church of England! Do not remain silent when it's *your* cause that is under threat in General Synod, and in our nation as a whole. May those who oppose your word be dismayed and put to shame, and know that you are God."

As the Psalmist prays in verse 16: "Cover their faces with shame, LORD, so that they will seek your name." Bring down the false pride and empty philosophies of our day, Lord – the moronic idiocy we see on TV and on social media. The arrogant regimes that suppress the gospel and oppress your people.

Bring down those who rise up against us, so that in disgrace and shame they will seek you out, and find that your word is true, and you alone are the Most High over all the earth. Not for our sake, but for God's own glory and fame.

We've seen some celebrity atheists declare recently that they have a fondness for "cultural Christianity". How lovely. I agree that the culture created by Christianity is a far better place to live than that created by other religions and ideologies. They think it's a blessing.

But Jesus is not just a great teacher to be admired. He is the Most High God, to be worshipped and adored. There is no cultural Christianity without people actually believing in and following Jesus.

So don't let them get away with it, Lord. Don't stand aloft.

We have a whiteboard on our fridge at home. And for a while now, I've had written on it the words of the second verse of the national anthem. I apply it to the enemies not of King Charles, but of King Jesus and his gospel. Changing the last words to "the church", it reflects the thoughts of Psalm 83, applied to our church today. Join me in praying:

O Lord our God arise,
scatter our enemies,
and make them fall!
Confound their politics,
frustrate their knavish tricks,
on Thee our hopes we fix,
God save the church

There is no cultural Christianity without people actually believing in and following Jesus.

Longing for God

Psalm 84

In Psalm 84, the psalmist turns to reflect on something far more positive than in Psalm 83: his experience of praising God with others in the Temple. Sometimes we think of the Psalms as a random collection of hymns and songs, one without much connection to the next, but maybe there is a good reason why this psalm comes hot on the heels of the dismay in Psalm 83. In the midst of many assaults and difficulties, we long for an end to the strife, and for a transforming encounter with the true presence of God.

Psalm 84

For the director of music. According to gittith. Of the Sons of Korah. A psalm.

How lovely is your dwelling place,
 LORD Almighty!
My soul yearns, even faints,
 for the courts of the LORD;
my heart and my flesh cry out
 for the living God.
Even the sparrow has found a home,
 and the swallow a nest for herself,
 where she may have her young—
a place near your altar,
 LORD Almighty, my King and my God.
Blessed are those who dwell in your house;
 they are ever praising you.

Blessed are those whose strength is in you,
 whose hearts are set on pilgrimage.
As they pass through the Valley of Baka,
 they make it a place of springs;

    the autumn rains also cover it with pools.
They go from strength to strength,
    till each appears before God in Zion.

Hear my prayer, LORD God Almighty;
    listen to me, God of Jacob.
Look on our shield, O God;
    look with favour on your anointed one.

Better is one day in your courts
    than a thousand elsewhere;
I would rather be a doorkeeper in the house of my God
    than dwell in the tents of the wicked.
For the LORD God is a sun and shield;
    the LORD bestows favour and honour;
no good thing does he withhold
    from those whose walk is blameless.

LORD Almighty,
    blessed is the one who trusts in you.

As Christopher Ash says, this psalm "breathes a warm desire for God and a rich delight in God."[1] He is the one we want, the one we turn to, when everything in the world around us is like Psalm 83.

We run home to our Beloved, and breath a sigh of relief and joy. With the turbulence of the storm outside, when all seems big and scary, even the smallest sparrow and most insignificant or vulnerable amongst us can find a home with him, and be safe.

As Psalm 84 verses 4 and 5 say:
> Blessed are those who dwell in your house;
>> they are ever praising you.
> Blessed are those whose strength is in you,
>> whose hearts are set on pilgrimage.

The only true blessing comes when people praise Jesus. When they put their trust in him and set their hearts on *pilgrimage*

---

1 Christopher Ash, *The Psalms: A Christ-Centered Commentary. Volume 3, Psalms 51-100* (Wheaton: Crossway, 2024), 411.

– following him as disciples, not just admiring the cultural by-products of the faith of others. Only then is it safe enough to sing with all our hearts. "How lovely is your dwelling place, LORD Almighty!"

Personal experience of God

This is the experience of many when they come across the Church at a local level: in our local churches we are near to God and feed on his word; we praise his name, and love his people. As verse 10 says, "I would rather be a doorkeeper in the house of my God than dwell in the tents of the wicked."

God is not absent. He has not abandoned us. Despite the negativity emanating from our national church institutions, and from various campaigning groups, here in many parishes there is real gospel joy.

At congregational level, there is so much to give thanks for in the Church. Many gospel churches are thriving; children are being brought up in the faith; new churches are being planted; old ones are being slowly revitalised.

There may be something of a "quiet revival" underway, according to a report from the Bible Society.[2] Sales of the Bible are apparently well up on recent years, showing an 87% increase over the last five years.[3] On Easter Sunday 2025 they were turning people away at St Aldate's in Oxford, I heard, and it was standing room only at St Ebbe's down the road. As I've travelled around the country recently, I've heard encouraging stories of baptisms and confirmations, new people turning up at churches, God being at work.

So even while we lament what is going on in the House of Bishops and in General Synod, it is simply not true that the Church of England is lifeless, dead, and over. While the gospel continues to be preached and

---

2 See Rhiannon Mcaleer and Rob Barward-Symmons, *The Quiet Revival* (Bible Society, 2025).

3 See Laura Barry, "Bible Sales Surge Among Gen Z" on the SPCK website www.spckpublishing.co.uk.

So even while we lament what is going on in the House of Bishops and in General Synod, it is simply not true that the Church of England is lifeless, dead, and over.

believed in so many of our churches, there is still hope and a future, however bleak some of the headlines may seem. We continue to seek his face in the midst of all the fog.

The valley of difficulty

Verse 6 says that as pilgrims to the temple pass through the Valley of Baka, they make it a place of springs. As God's people go through a dry place or a vale of tears, they transform it, and bring it life and health. Nothing will stop them from getting to God, from being with him. Ain't no mountain high enough or arid desert hot enough to keep them from him.

The sixteenth-century Reformer, Martin Luther (1483-1546) once said he was grateful to God for his theological opponents, because they made him a better theologian in the midst of their disagreements. I am, he said, "deeply indebted to my papists that through the devil's raging they have beaten, oppressed, and distressed me so much. That is to say, they have made a fairly good theologian of me, which I would not have become otherwise." As soon as God's word takes root in someone, the devil starts pestering them, and makes a real theologian out of them because his assaults teach us to seek and love God's word.[4] St Augustine (354-430) also said Christians could benefit even from a time of great theological turmoil; he wrote:

> *"For while the hot restlessness of heretics stirs questions about many articles of the catholic [universal] faith, the necessity of defending them forces us both to investigate them more accurately, to understand them more clearly, and to proclaim them more earnestly; and the question mooted by an adversary becomes the occa-*

---

4 Martin Luther, *Luther's Works, Vol. 34: Career of the Reformer IV* (ed. Jaroslav Jan Pelikan, Hilton C. Oswald, and Helmut T. Lehmann; Philadelphia: Fortress Press, 1999), 287.

sion of instruction."[5]

Now, don't mishear me. Heresy is a bad thing. Heresy attempts to rob Christ of his glory and his authority – a theft which no true Christian can endure. But it can also have beneficial side-effects, if we use it as an opportunity to learn. If we use it to go deeper into God and enjoy him for who he really is. Then we pass through that desert, that Valley of Baka, and make it a place of refreshment.

This has happened in England. As the enemies of the gospel bear down on those of us in the Church of England, we have found a new sense of unity with others who also know God our Saviour, and call on him out of a pure heart (2 Timothy 2:22). The "hot restlessness of heretics" has brought clarity and solidarity to gospel people across the Church.

---

[5] P. Schaff (ed.), *St. Augustin's City of God and Christian Doctrine* (Nicene and Post-Nicene Fathers, First Series, Volume 2. Translated by M. Dods; Peabody, Massachusetts: Hendrickson, 1999), 309-310.

We are now working together more than I have ever known — not without discernment and care, but also not without many benefits. In our gospel coalitions and alliances, we go "from strength to strength" as the Psalm puts it in verse 7.

We can have sweet fellowship together, praising God for the common faith that brings us together at a time of uncertainty and difficulty.

The Son rises in the wilderness

In Psalm 83 before, we had a prayer for God to listen up, and do something about our enemies. Now in Psalm 84 verse 8, we have another prayer.

> Hear my prayer, LORD God Almighty;
> > listen to me, God of Jacob.
> Look on our shield, O God;
> > look with favour on your anointed one.

Give us strength for the journey, he prays. Don't let anything keep us from you, and hold us back.

But what's this request to look on our shield, and look with favour on "your anointed one"? It sounds like a prayer for the anointed king. "God save the king", as it were. We know from Psalm 2 that the rulers of the world band together against the LORD and against his anointed king. So are they praying here for God to help their king, in the context of the previous psalm when everything seems against them?

But this is a psalm by "the Sons of Korah", in Book 3 of the Psalms. Most of the prayers in this part of Psalms "express sorrow and pain at the strained relationship between God and his people."[6] Probably because the people are in exile, away from the land, and without an actual king.

Things are not going well in this section of the book of Psalms:

---

[6] Nancy Declaissé-Walford, Rolf A. Jacobson, and Beth Laneel Tanner, *The Book of Psalms* (NICOT; Grand Rapids: Eerdmans, 2014), 654.

- Psalm 74 lamented the destruction of the sanctuary, the temple, "these everlasting ruins". The enemies of Israel mocked God, and there were no prophets left.

- Psalm 79 howls in pain that the nations have invaded the land and defiled the temple, reducing Jerusalem to rubble.

- Psalm 89 is confused. God, you said we would always have a king in the line of David on our throne, forever, to be our shield. But you've rejected and spurned us, and "been very angry *with your anointed one*", it says (89:38).

It looks like the covenant has been renounced, the kings have gone, and the crown and shield have been defiled. So the context in this whole section of the Psalms is national disaster and the apparent end of the covenant with king David. Maybe that's why Psalm 84 verse 3 says God himself is our King. He is all they have left. He is their only hope.

But still, it also says in verse 9: "Look on our shield… Look with favour on your anointed one."

It could mean, we know you're our king, Lord. But restore the fortunes of the House of David too. Bring back the good times for our kings. And then we will rejoice again, and everything will be fine. The nation is dead. What we need is a resurrection! Look with favour on your anointed one.

But is this just a political hope, a longing for a great leader to restore the nation's fortunes and make us great again?

Of course, that phrase "anointed one" can also be translated "messiah". Or in the Greek translation, it says, "look on the face of your Christ." That's our only hope. That God will look on the face of his Christ, and give us a resurrection. So we can praise him again in the midst of national catastrophe.

Access to God depends entirely on Christ, our temple, and on the Father's favour to

The world gives us empty promises, but we have an empty tomb, full of promise.

wards him. Unless God our Father brings Christ back from the dead, we can't enjoy a single day in his presence. All we would have is "a thousand elsewhere" – in the tents of the wicked, away from the glory and the safety of the courts of his temple, in hell.

But hope is exactly what we do have, in Christ. God does not dwell in temples made by human hands, but "in Christ all the fulness of the Deity lives in bodily form." (Colossians 2:9).

Our Christ is risen – he is risen indeed, Hallelujah!

And where his people gather together, he assures us he is there in the midst of them (Matthew 18:20). As someone put it, the world gives us empty promises, but we have an empty tomb, full of promise.

Because Psalm 84 verse 11 says, "For the LORD God is a sun and shield." The Lord himself is our shield and our king: Christ, the risen Lord.

As the old hymn put it:

> *"Hail the heav'n-born Prince of Peace!*
>
> *Hail the Sun of righteousness!*
>
> *Light and life to all He brings,*
>
> *Ris'n with healing in His wings."*

So if we long for God's presence in the midst of a national calamity, it is to Christ alone that we must turn. When everything around us seems dangerous and dark, blessed is the one who trusts in him. In Christ we enjoy every spiritual blessing in the heavenly realms (Ephesians 1:3).

So say it boldly – because every hope we have depends on this:

Christ is risen!

He is risen indeed – hallelujah!

And join with me in prayer:

Lord Almighty, Most High over all the earth
   our King and our God,
   our sun and our shield,
   who brought back from the dead our Lord Jesus,
   the great shepherd of the sheep
   by the blood of the eternal covenant:

Give us grace, in the midst of so many troubles
   in church, and state, and around the globe,

That we may so long for your presence in this dangerous world,
   that the enemies of the gospel would be ashamed and dismayed,

and turn to you in repentance and faith,
   and the whole earth resound with your praise;

For we ask in the powerful name of Jesus,
   who is alive, and reigns with you and the Holy Spirit,
   One God, now and forever,

Amen.

Praying for Glory

Psalm 85

Psalms 83 and 84 are important context for Psalm 85, which helps to guide and inform our prayers for the church in this country right now. We have seen so far how the people of God were under attack, from outside enemies, false brethren, and the forces of unbelief. And yet, in Psalm 84, it is lovely to be in his presence, amongst his people. He is our God and our King, our sun, and our shield.

So now we turn to Psalm 85. If Psalm 84 was about an individual, yearning for a revitalised life and a relationship with God; Psalm 85 is about the same thing, but for the church as a whole. It is a prayer for God's glory to return to the land.

Psalm 85

For the director of music. Of the Sons of Korah. A psalm.

You, LORD, showed favour to your land;
    you restored the fortunes of Jacob.
You forgave the iniquity of your people
    and covered all their sins.
You set aside all your wrath
    and turned from your fierce anger.

Restore us again, God our Saviour,
    and put away your displeasure toward us.
Will you be angry with us forever?
    Will you prolong your anger through all generations?
Will you not revive us again,
    that your people may rejoice in you?
Show us your unfailing love, LORD,
    and grant us your salvation.

I will listen to what God the LORD says;
    he promises peace to his people, his faithful ser-

vants—
>   but let them not turn to folly.
> Surely his salvation is near those who fear him,
>   that his glory may dwell in our land.
>
> Love and faithfulness meet together;
>   righteousness and peace kiss each other.
> Faithfulness springs forth from the earth,
>   and righteousness looks down from heaven.
> The LORD will indeed give what is good,
>   and our land will yield its harvest.
> Righteousness goes before him
>   and prepares the way for his steps.

Remembering past forgiveness

The psalmist begins by remembering what God had done in the past for his people when they were at a low ebb. Psalm 85 verse 1: "You, Lord, showed favour to your land; you restored the fortunes of Jacob".

The Psalmist recalls the way in which God had revived and restored his people previously when things had not been going well; how he had turned from his fierce anger in disciplining them, and restored their fortunes and his favour.

Because his favour had been withdrawn, and the fortunes of the people had taken a turn for the worst. They were sinful, and he was angry. He cannot be placid and calm when *his* righteousness confronts *our* unfaithfulness. He is the moral arbiter of the universe. We look to him, to know what is right and wrong. And when we are in the wrong, he is angry.

But the psalmist recalls a time when God

restored the fortunes of his people. He forgave the inquity of all their sins, and set aside all his righteous wrath. He turned from his fierce anger. And they were glad!

I should just mention, that when it says in verse 2 that God covered all their sins, that doesn't mean he "covered them up", as we say. As Psalm 32 will tell us, if we just cover things up like that, with no repentance, and hope no-one will find out, it only saps our strength and dries us up.

God doesn't "cover up" for our sins, like someone trying to distract attention from misdemeanours or hide the evidence of bad behaviour. He doesn't cover up and conceal the truth in that sense.

No. What it means is, he's got it covered. That is, he makes atonement for it. Atonement that somehow also turns away his own anger and wrath.

This is why a time of revival is a time of rejoicing in sins forgiven. And a time for rejoicing in what Jesus did on the cross.

There is no forgiveness in our current cancel culture. No way back into favour. Even if you do *I'm a Celebrity Get Me Out of Here* and disappear into a jungle to eat unspeakable things like they do (in the hope they will be reinstated into the public's favour), rehabilitation for those who have been "cancelled" is nigh on impossible in our society.

But in Christ, there is true forgiveness. From *all* our sins. A lightening of the load, a freedom from the burden, a leaping for joy.

Revival is not increasing numbers, or improving church finances, or greater prestige and influence. It is exuberant joy at sins forgiven, because God has turned away his anger.

He gave us up to our sins, and the consequences of our sins. But in his mercy, he sent his Son, to die in our place on the cross, to reconcile the Father to us. Revival

Revival is not increasing numbers, or improving church finances, or greater prestige and influence. It is exuberant joy at sins forgiven, because God has turned away his anger.

in the church will always have the cross at its heart. The blood of Christ, shed for me, that I can go free.

Revival comes to a church that knows it needs forgiveness. That knows God is rightly angry at their sins. We confess them openly. And yet in his mercy, he has forgotten them. As far as the east is from the west, so far has he removed our sins from us (Psalm 103:12). They are nailed to the tree, for you and for me.

It's only because of the cross, that God can revive us again. Only because of his mercy and grace, which we could never earn or deserve or merit in any way.

Remembering past revivals

So this psalm starts by saying, "Hey! Lord! You did this in the past. You revived us when we were down and out. And it was great."

Such revivals of the church can be seen in

the pages of the Bible itself. God rescued his people from many hostile adversaries in the era of the Judges. Some of those rescues are alluded to in Psalm 83.

God revived his people in the days of good king Josiah, when God's word was rediscovered and everything was reformed. He brought them back from exile in Babylon; he protected and strengthened them in the time of Ezra and Nehemiah, when his name and his word were honoured and heeded.

It's not clear if the psalmist has one of these moments particularly in mind, so we can surely repurpose the general idea.

The enemies of God's people back in Psalm 83 – Edom, the Ishmaelites, Moab and the Hagrites – no-one has even heard of them now. No-one follows Zeeb or Zalmunna now, or honours their names. They are the ones who have disappeared into the mists of time, not the persecuted church of the living God, which continues to grow and flourish around the world. They did not succeed in their plots.

Like the Khmer Rouge and Pol Pot did not succeed in their infamous plots to wipe out the church in Cambodia during the 1970s. The church they attempted so vigorously to wipe out and destroy is now flourishing, with hundreds of thousands of members. God renewed and revived them because, as the early church father, Tertullian (160-240) put it, "The oftener we are mown down by you, the more in number we grow; the blood of Christians is seed."[1] Or, as Augustine said, the church is "fertilized richly with the blood of the martyrs".[2]

We have also seen revivals in England too.

---

[1] Tertullian, *The Apology*, chapter 50 in *Latin Christianity: Its Founder, Tertullian*, ed. Alexander Roberts, James Donaldson, and A. Cleveland Coxe, trans. S. Thelwall, vol. 3 of *The Ante-Nicene Fathers* (Buffalo, NY: Christian Literature Company, 1885), 55.

[2] Augustine of Hippo, *The City of God*, 22.7.1 in *St. Augustine's City of God and Christian Doctrine*, ed. Philip Schaff, trans. Marcus Dods, vol. 2 of *A Select Library of the Nicene and Post-Nicene Fathers of the Christian Church, First Series* (Buffalo, NY: Christian Literature Company, 1887), 484.

The Lord restored our spiritual fortunes through the work of men such as John Wycliffe and William Tyndale, and great bishops like Cranmer, Ridley, and Latimer during the Reformation. They saved us from superstition, gave us back the Bible, and helped us worship and pray to God, all in our own language.[3]

Those reformers and revivers died for their faith – except Wycliffe, of course, who was only burnt at the stake after he'd been dead for 30 years. But revival came in his wake all the same. By the time they had dug up his rotting corpse and burned it, sprinkling his ashes into the River Swift near Lutterworth, the word of God was flowing out to the people again, in a language they could understand. As Basil the Great (330-378) once put it, "the blood of the martyrs, watering the Churches, nourished many more champions of true religion."[4]

---

3 See Lee Gatiss, *Light After Darkness: How the Reformers Regained, Retold, and Relied on the Gospel of Grace* (Fearn: Christian Focus, 2019).

4 Basil of Caesarea, Letter CLXIV to Ascholius in *St. Basil:*

God showed favour to England *again*, in the Evangelical Revivals of the eighteenth century through the preaching of George Whitefield (1714-1770) and others, and the labours of great women such as Selina Hastings, the Countess of Huntingdon (1707-1791). Thousands gathered in the open air, in the rain even, to hear the gospel of sins forgiven. Churches were filled again and many were saved.

And God poured out his blessings upon our nation – and the world – through the evangelical endeavours of William Wilberforce (1759-1833) and the 7th Earl of Shaftesbury (1801-1885) and Hannah More (1745-1833) in the nineteenth century. Slaves and children were emancipated by those who knew the joy of a relationship with Christ and were convinced he was coming back.

Letters and Select Works, ed. Philip Schaff and Henry Wace, trans. Blomfield Jackson, vol. 8 of *A Select Library of the Nicene and Post-Nicene Fathers of the Christian Church, Second Series* (New York: Christian Literature Company, 1895), 216.

There is a church building in every village, town, and city of this land, as a testimony to how he has been at work amongst us over the last two millennia.

The gospel went out around the world with our growing trade, and though missionaries often again paid the ultimate price, the fertile soil was filled with gospel seed, which flowers to this day throughout the Anglican Communion and beyond.

There is a church building in every village, town, and city of this land, as a testimony to how he has been at work amongst us over the last two millennia. The gospel grows in many foreign lands because of what God did in and through England.God has been here. He has been active. Millions have rejoiced in the forgiveness he brings, and sung songs about the old rugged cross where Jesus died to save us.

And it was great.

It WAS great.

Restore us again

But this is not simply nostalgia for a bygone era. Because Psalm 85 quickly shifts to lament and yearning. After recalling God's favour felt in the past, in verses 1-3, now verses 4-6 express a perceived sense of God's present displeasure and a desire for restored favour and joy:

> "Restore us <u>again</u>, God our Saviour,
> and put away your displeasure toward us.
> Will you be angry with us forever?"

It used to be great. You did amazing things, Lord. Now do it again. *Please* do it again.

Because it isn't great now. We feel God's displeasure. We feel his anger. We have little to rejoice in, it seems, with the way things are going in our world.

Not just poverty, war, and injustice, and the crazy things our global leaders do and say. But the famine of God's word, the struggle against his truth, and the persecution of his people, which are all too common today.

Is this how it's always going to be from now on? "Will you prolong your anger through all generations?" We never knew we had it so good, and now it just isn't anymore. Is it ever likely to be so again?

This harmonises with concerns within the Church of England about declining attendance, changing demographics, political paralysis, and our perceived cultural irrelevance.

The gospel is choked on every side, and few will give their lives to serve it here anymore, on arid soil in a hostile environment. The Church of England needs at least six hundred new ministers every year, to remain a national church. There are three Anglican ordinands studying in the first year at Oak Hill Theological College in London. Only three. Other theological colleges are hardly bursting at the seams either.[5]

Where are the men who will step up to

---

5 In 2024–2025, the number of ordinands in residential training for ministry at all of the Church of England's theological colleges combined is only sixty-five. We have an acute vocations crisis.

preach the living word of God in our churches? Pretty soon, we won't have any to fill the gaps when the current clergy retire. We won't be able to maintain gospel ministry in our existing evangelical churches, never mind to revitalise others or start something new.

The cry, "Will you not revive us again?" becomes a prayer for a reawakening of faith and purpose, in the nation and in its established church.

This plea for revival resonates with the longing of many within the Church for a fresh outpouring of the Holy Spirit, a revitalization of spiritual life, and a renewal of authentic faith.

What we need above all is not political victories in the arena of General Synod, which is so often just a polemical pantomime performance. Such victories would be welcome. But what we really need is a rejuvenated relationship with God, a rekindled passion for his word, and a revivified mission to the confused and lost people of this broken and polarised island.

They need the gospel of God our Saviour, as much as ever. But who wants to hear it, and who wants to tell them about it, anymore?

"O that you would rend the heavens and come down!" as Isaiah 64:1 so poignantly prays. We need God himself to act, and not continue to give us over, in his justice, to the effects of our own sins.

> "Show us your unfailing love, LORD,
> and grant us your salvation."

It needs to be something that *he* does, that *he* grants. Nothing we do can make this happen. It doesn't happen because we're worthy enough, or because we have some special status, some peculiar merit. We don't.

We're only haunted by the uncomfortable memory of once having been a baptised nation, which has not added true faith to

What we really need is a rejuvenated relationship with God, a rekindled passion for his word, and a revivified mission to the confused and lost people of this broken and polarised island.

the promises once made. The weight of the privilege and responsibility that rests on us, the obligation that presses so insistently because of all the spiritual blessings we have enjoyed from God in the past, only aggravates our sin as we blindly try, as a nation, to ignore it.

And now the ghost of nominal Christianity has been almost completely driven out by a post-modern secularism and an expressive individualism which cares little for Jesus, and the good news he brings. And the consequent signs of his displeasure are all around us in England today.

Judgment on the church

What is actually happening with the church? While our generation is seeking clarity on crucial moral and spiritual issues, we in the church are going through a time of judgment. Quite apart from the recent pandemic and the current challenges to our nation's economy and health, we have moral confusion, poor leadership, false teaching, no sense of direction, and what the prophet Amos called "a famine of the word of the Lord" (Amos 8:11).

These are tell-tale signs of a nation and a church under the heavy hand of God, who (as the prophet Malachi put it) threatens to curse our blessings (Malachi 2:1-9). Yes, he will curse those "blessings" that we talk so much about.

We've got antisemitism tolerated on our streets, racist attitudes on our screens, creeping censorship in our schools. We had one of the worst harvests in 2024 since records began, and how long before war becomes a present reality on these shores and not just far away across the oceans, at arms length? Not to mention the Parliamentary attempts to expand the culture of death to include not just the unborn, but the aged and depressed as well.

It ought to make us grieve more, and pray.

But all the while, we have indulgent lethargy encouraged on our sofas, as we scroll through endless superficialities. All of these things are indicators of a profound generational malaise.

> "Will you not revive us again,
> that your people may rejoice in you?
> Show us your unfailing love, LORD,
> and grant us your salvation."

Judgment begins with the household of God, as the apostle Peter said. So even our evangelical world has been rocked by various exposés and scandals of late. This is an answer to prayer, so that we too might be purified as part of this divine refining.

We evangelicals are not immune from God's judgment – because we are not as sanctified and special as we may comfortingly have assumed ourselves to be.

We are under God's judgment, as much as anybody else. We have followed too much the devices and desires of our own hearts.

We have left undone what we ought to have done, and done what ought not to be done. We must acknowledge and bewail our manifold sins and wickedness, which we from time to time most grievously have committed by thought and word and deed, provoking most justly God's wrath and indignation against us.

Have we applied our gospel to our relationships with the church at large, and been good news to all our neighbours? Or have we just kept our heads down in the parish? Have we been too comfortable with our easy chairs and easy answers, drugged by our own melodies so we're oblivious to the drumbeats outside the walls of the churchyard?

Does anything stretch in our churches anymore, except maybe our elasticated waistbands?

We have left unchallenged some things that should be challenged, and not spoken out about some of our spokesmen.

Does God care about our accents, our schooling, and that of our leaders; how good the after-service coffee is, how padded the pew cushions, and how professional the music and sound system and slides are? Or does he care about the widow, the orphan, and the immigrant – the least, the last, and the lost – the confused and bewildered generation that we have been called to serve?

Has our agenda been God's agenda?

Not always.

And so we have been ashamed and embarrassed and dismayed, as God has brought into the light some of the shocking things which have been hidden, in report after report after report.

It's not just evangelicals of course. Not all the abusers are from one particular part of the church. Every party has to recruit its leaders from the same fallen human race. But we must bear our own guilt. We have been shamed.

I have often asked: Why have you done this now, Lord? Why, when we need to be strong and together to counter all the false teaching and lack of belief, do we have to endure all the scandals in our own ranks? All the negative publicity and people caught up in the scandals with Zacharias, Pilavachi, Sizer, Smyth, Fletcher. And others.

Bad timing, Lord! You've undermined our cause and made us look bad, just when we needed to be at the top of our game. Couldn't you just have got them on judgment day? Or twenty years ago? Why *now*, with so much atheism and heresy for us to contend with? What kind of providence is this?

And you know what God says? He says, I forgive sin. I sent my Son to die for your sin. But I'm not here to cover up for you, or make *you* look good. I'm not interested in your cause, but mine. And my purpose in everything is to glorify my name, and work all things for good, for those who love me.

If revival is to come, it will glorify the name of Jesus, not the name of your celebrities and organisations.

> "I am God and there is no other." (Isaiah 46:9)
>
> "I will not yield my glory to another." (Isaiah 48:11)

If revival is to come, it can only be because of God's unfailing love and sovereign grace, not because of our methods and ministries and men.

Maybe we needed that reminder. Maybe we always do.

What does the Lord require of us? To build grand and shiny churches and organisations that we think are too big and important to fail? The Lord laughs at our folly. He wants us to act justly, and love mercy, and walk humbly with our God (Micah 6:8). Only then may our examples influence others and draw them to Christ. As Jonathan Edwards (1703-1758) observed during the

What does the Lord require of us? To build grand and shiny churches and organisations that we think are too big and important to fail? The Lord laughs at our folly.

revivals of the eighteenth century, "There never yet was a time of remarkable pouring out of the Spirit, and great revival of religion, but that example had a main hand."[6]

I don't know if the "quiet revival" some have spoken about will become louder and noisier. I pray that it does, and that it isn't simply a by-product of the current breeze in the West away from progressive politics and back towards a cultural conservatism. I hope it has greater spiritual roots and spiritual fruit than that. But either way, it has not come about because of our worthiness, and will not be fostered by our supposed brilliance.

It may even happen almost entirely outside of "our circles", and yet still be a true revival. As someone commented during the evangelical awakening of the eighteenth century, "I hope none dislike the work, because they have not been used as instruments of

---

[6] Jonathan Edwards, *Jonathan Edwards on Revival* (Edinburgh: Banner of Truth, 1965), 99 from his book *The Distinguishing Marks of a Work of the Spirit of God* (1741).

it. For if we love our Lord Jesus Christ in sincerity, we shall rejoice to see him increase, though we should decrease."[7] The Church of England has been greatly used by God for his glory in the past. But it may yet still shrink and die; though if the gospel grows and is honoured regardless, it doesn't really matter.

Maybe the fact that God has been humbling his own people is a sign that he has not forgotten or abandoned us, and still wants to use us for his purposes in this land? Maybe his power is made perfect through weakness (2 Corinthians 12:9). Maybe we are being pruned like a vine, in the hope of greater fruitfulness (John 15:1-2).

Let us pray that there emerges from these ashes, a deep personal and corporate repentance, so we are ready to rebuild after the earthquake and fire.

---

[7] William Cooper's preface to Jonathan Edwards's *Distinguishing Marks* in Edwards, *Jonathan Edwards on Revival*, 83.

Preparing the way for God's feet

Psalm 85 gives us some pointers for the way forward, if we truly long for revival. Verse 8 says,

> "I will listen to what God the LORD says;
>
> he promises peace to his people, his faithful servants–
>
> but let them not turn to folly."

This is the way to revival – listen to what God the LORD says. Embrace his promises and faithfully follow his commands. This is the path to peace, and renewal.

But at the same time, those who faithfully confess his name must "not turn to folly" themselves. God does not bless goofiness or ungodliness.

When revival comes, as verses 10 and 11 of the psalm put it, "Love and faithfulness meet together; righteousness and peace kiss each other. Faithfulness springs forth from the earth, and righteousness looks

Those who faithfully confess his name must "not turn to folly" themselves. God does not bless goofiness or ungodliness.

down from heaven." And as verses 12 and 13 say:

> The LORD will indeed give what is good,
>   and our land will yield its harvest.

BUT….

> Righteousness goes before him
>   and prepares the way for his steps.

Revival may follow the period of judgment we are experiencing, if God in his sovereign mercy so chooses. But perhaps only as we prepare the way, by seeking to amend the mistakes of the past and put our own house in order.

Righteousness prepares the way for his steps. It's not mechanical, like "input righteousness here, and get revival there." It's a way of showing the fruits of repentance and faith. Showing we really do want God's way to return. We want God to step in, for his feet to walk upon England's mountains green again, as they apparently did in ancient times.

We want God to step in, for his feet to walk upon England's mountains green again, as they apparently did in ancient times.

If we really desire the abundant blessings he wants to pour out upon us in his goodness and mercy, it won't just mean more people coming into our churches to make us feel better, make us feel more important, part of something bigger and more impressive. It will mean more humility, more light shining in dark places, and more putting things right. It won't necessarily seem like a time of great excitement, but a time of brokenness, repentance, and deep concern for the salvation of souls.

"Will you not revive us again?"

For the glory of God and the good of England, please join me in praying for this kind of revival.

Let's pray.

Heavenly Father, God our Saviour,
   you showed favour to your people in the Old Testament,
   and have repeatedly forgiven the iniquity of the people of England.

In the cross of the Lord Jesus Christ,
   you set aside all your wrath, so we could know peace.

Restore us again, and put away your displeasure with us, which we feel every day and see on the news and in our streets.

Do not prolong your anger through all generations.

Show us your unfailing love and grant us your salvation.

Help us listen to what you say, and not turn to folly,
   that we may fear you, and walk in righteousness and faithfulness.
   so your glory will again dwell with us,

For the everlasting fame of Jesus, our king.

In whose name we pray, Amen.

Gospel Flourishing in a Time of Confusion

This book addresses key questions facing Anglican Evangelicals at this moment of confusion and uncertainty. Should we stay in the Church of England, and make use of the many gospel opportunities it affords? Or should we leave for pastures new, since things within the established church have become so difficult? What does it mean to be a "righteous remnant" in an apostate church, when everyone seems to be doing "what is right in their own eyes"? And are there lessons we can learn from how our ancestors handled these sorts of questions, not just in recent times but in the very earliest days of the church?

Five bishops, pastors, and theologians offer here a resource to help us think through the issues, that the gospel of Jesus might flourish and spread in our nation.

www.churchsociety.org * admin@churchsociety.org

FIGHT VALIANTLY

What does it mean "to contend for the faith that was once for all delivered to the saints"? With so much confusion and argument in today's church, how are Christians meant to think about and react to false teaching? How can we promote the gospel lovingly in a context of opposition?

"We don't like contending, but sometimes faithfulness to Christ requires that we must. This book helpfully takes us to the Bible to show us why and how. An excellent resource for individuals, PCC members, and whole churches."

> Vaughan Roberts, Rector of St Ebbe's Oxford

Available from Church Society
www.churchsociety.org
admin@churchsociety.org

PB, 292 pages
ISBN: 9781739937645

Handel's Messiah has captivated audiences for centuries, but the depth of its theological and spiritual messages invites deeper exploration. In A Month with the Messiah, a cast of thirty scholars, pastors, musicians, and theologians come together to provide a profound and accessible devotional commentary on this musical masterpiece. Curated to appeal both to longtime admirers and newcomers, this book dives into the libretto's scriptural themes with clarity and reverence.

This beautifully produced hardback companion to the Messiah invites readers on a journey of spiritual reflection, exploring the hope, redemption, and joy that Handel's music captures so vividly. Each contributor brings a unique perspective, drawing from their rich backgrounds to shed light on how these passages resonate in today's world.

Whether you're enjoying Messiah for the first time or looking to deepen your appreciation of it, this collection is a companion to enrich your listening, worship, and reflection on Handel's enduring work.

Order direct from Church Society:
www.churchsociety.org
admin@churchsociety.org

Church Society

EQUIPPING GOD'S
PEOPLE TO LIVE
GOD'S WORD

offering strategic leadership

For more than 180 years, Church Society has been contending to reform and renew the Church of England in biblical faith, on the basis of its Reformed foundations as expressed in the doctrine of the Articles, the worship of the Prayer Book, and the ministry of the Ordinal.

To find out more and to join Church Society, please visit our website, churchsociety.org

resourcing today's church

Church Society publishes several new books each year, bringing the best of our Anglican Evangelical heritage to new generations, and responding to new pressures and opportunities in today's Church and nation. We also produce a weekly podcast, a quarterly magazine and a theological journal, as well as our regular blog.

serving tomorrow's church

As part of our commitment to raising up a new generation of leaders, we host the annual Junior Anglican Evangelical Conference for those in the early stages of ministry. Church Society also has patronage of around 130 parishes, helping to protect evangelical ministry in the Church of England for the future.

www.ingramcontent.com/pod-product-compliance
Lightning Source LLC
Chambersburg PA
CBHW050330010526
44119CB00050B/737